SCHIRMER'S LIBRARY OF MUSICAL CLASSICS

Vol. 780

MUZIO CLEMENTI

Gradus ad Parnassum

Twenty-Nine Selected Studies

To which are added Scales in Thirds
in All Major and Minor Keys

Revised, Fingered and Annotated
by
CARL TAUSIG

With a Preface by
C. F. WEITZMANN

English Translation by
DR. TH. BAKER

G. SCHIRMER, Inc.

DISTRIBUTED BY

7777 W. BLUEMOUND RD. P.O. BOX 13819 MILWAUKEE, WI 53213

GRADUS AD PARNASSUM

PREFACE

Muzio Clementi, the originator of the brilliant piano-style of composition and of virtuosoship in piano-playing, was also the head of a School, the excellence of whose principles is still attested and exemplified by its disciples and following. His sonatas, which belong to the greater forms of composition, were so perfectly adapted to the character of the instrument for which they were intended, besides setting the player's artistic ability in a most favorable light, that they thenceforward stood for the type of all similar works. But his last work, published in 1817, the "Gradus ad Parnassum, or, The Art of Piano-playing Taught in One Hundred Examples," is likewise his *magnum opus*, by which he has assured his name, for all time, a prominent place in the history of the literature of his art. It is founded on the wide experience of a thorough, conscientious, and stimulating teacher; and no work has since appeared which surpasses it in many-sidedness and practical value. A student who has thoroughly practised the pieces in the "Gradus ad Parnassum" and can play them confidently and fluently, has thereby acquired the ability to execute the piano-works of all the masters from C. Ph. E. Bach down to Beethoven, without meeting with further substantial impediments. Many a disciple of art, however, has been disheartened by the great number of studies in the aforesaid work, devoted not only to the repetition of similar passages, styles of technique, and embellishments, but also including some pieces not in accord with modern taste.

For this reason the editor of the present edition made a selection of the most practical and profitable studies in the Gradus, comprising those calculated for mastering the most various difficulties, arranging them in progressive order and providing them with variants for fingering and interpretation ; thus undoubtedly meeting present requirements. He changed the original fingering only in passages where it no longer conforms to modern standards in this branch of piano-technics, or where the new fingering aims at strengthening fingers of either hand which are naturally weak, at training the several fingers in turning over or under, at increasing the stretching capacity of the hand, etc. Hence, an intelligent teacher will soon recognize the expediency of these more difficult fingerings, whether specially devised or intentionally selected ; more particularly because most of these numbers afford the student sufficient opportunity to maintain and increase his proficiency by employing the easiest fingering.

Clementi, the estimable author of these Studies, which are a *sine qua non* for every pianist, was born in 1752 at Rome, where he early began his musical education. In his eighteenth year he excelled all the pianists of his time by his spirited, virile and brilliant performances. His piano-style was popularized by artistic tours over the greater part of Europe, and with equal success through his numerous pupils of both sexes. When only in his ninth year he passed an examination for a position as organist in Rome ; in his twenty-ninth year he was invited by the Emperor to compete at Vienna with the illustrious Mozart in piano-playing and improvisation ; and at the ripe old age of eighty he was still capable of evoking the warmest enthusiasm at London, in an assembly of his pupils and admirers, among whom were J. B. Cramer and Ignaz Moscheles, by a free fantasia on the pianoforte.

Mozart, to be sure, who was prejudiced against all Italians, describes Clementi as a mere "mechanic," who shone in passages of thirds, but who did not possess a pennyworth of feeling or taste. But Ludwig Berger, one of Clementi's most distinguished pupils, published in the "Cecilia" for 1829 (Vol. 10, p. 200) an explanation of Mozart's harsh opinion of his revered master. He put the question to Clementi, whether he had played at that early period (1781) in his present (1806) piano-style. Clementi replied in the negative, adding "that at the time mentioned he had a peculiar predilection for great brilliancy of execution, especially for extempore performances and passages in double-notes, which latter were unknown before his time ; not until later had he acquired a more songful and noble style of playing from attentively listening to celebrated singers of the time, also aided by the gradual improvement of the English grand pianofortes in particular, whose former imperfect construction rendered a really smooth and singing execution almost impossible." "Thus it seems to me," continues Berger, "that Mozart's opinion, which characterizes Clementi as lacking both taste and feeling, and which can, therefore give rise only to misconstructions hurtful to Mozart, is after all, to a certain extent, natural. But it does not in the least affect or disparage the later, and generally recognized, creator and perfecter of the elegant style of piano-playing."

Clementi's other pupils, among whom Field, Klengel, Cramer and Bertini deserve special eulogy, also expressed themselves at all times with equal enthusiasm concerning the animated playing and the stimulating instructive method of their master, whom they often accompanied on concert-tours through England, France, Germany, Russia and Italy.

As remarked above, the "Gradus ad Parnassum" is Clementi's most important work for pianoforte, and elaborated with peculiar devotion and care. The numbers which it contains, and more especially those found in this selection, are Studies in the true sense of the term. For each of them treats either some special figure, or rolling or undulating passages, broken chords, some purposely selected difficulty, or some other motive calculated to make the fingers independent, or to develop the player's agility, strength and endurance ; working out the motives in the most various forms, with changes of position and modulations, throughout the piece. They will, in consequence, enable the student who can execute them with confidence and fluency to play with ease similar runs and passages in the works of other composers, and besides to acquire the confidence, clearness and routine requisite for the performance of any species of composition.

In the editor's opinion, only Clementi and Chopin have written Studies which are perfectly adapted to the above end. He employs them as chief instruction-books in the School of Advanced Piano-playing* conducted by himself, and also for his own practice. Thus Clementi, by means of this series, has provided a key with which the student can unlock the entire literature of the piano from J. S. Bach (who requires, however, specialized study) down to Beethoven ; while Chopin's Studies prepare the way from Beethoven to Liszt, in whose compositions virtuosity soars to dizzy heights.

C. F. WEITZMANN.

*Tausig's "Schule des höheren Klavierspiels," an academy which he conducted in Berlin from 1865 to 1870. [Translator.]

4

Veloce.

1.

*)Alle Noten werden gleichmässig stark angeschlagen. Diese Etüde soll gebunden und gestossen geübt werden.
**) Der Übergang von der weissen zur schwarzen Taste darf nicht wahrgenommen werden.

*) Attaquez chaque note avec une même égalité de force. Exercez cette étude legato et staccato.
**) Le passage d'une touche blanche à une touche noire doit s'effectuer sans que l'on s'en aperçoive.

*) Strike all the notes with equal force. This Étude should be practised both *legato* and *staccato*.
**) The passage from the white key to the black should be effected smoothly.

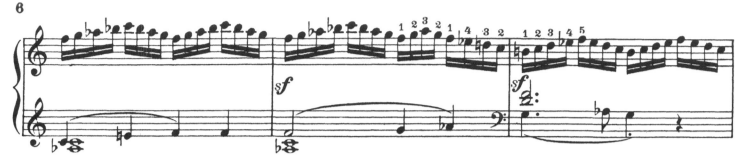

2.

Veloce.

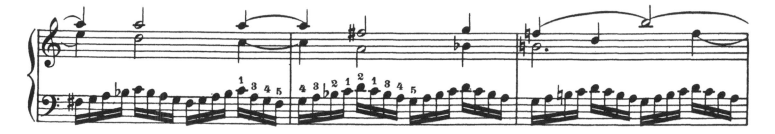

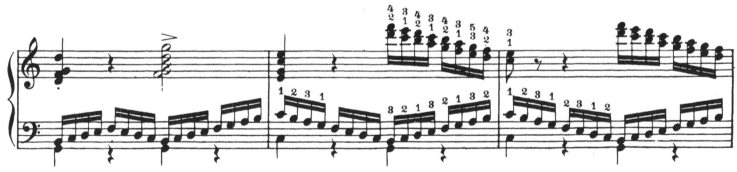

3.

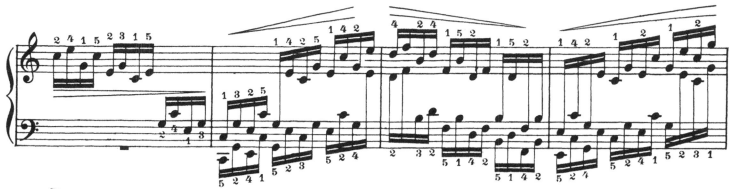

*) Die Passagen sollen mit solcher Schärfe und Deutlichkeit articulirt werden, dass sie fast den Eindruck eines sehr feinen und leichten Staccatos machen.

*) *Pour avoir l'impression d'un staccato léger et délicat, il faut exécuter ces passages avec une grande clarté et une parfaite netteté.*

*) The passages should be articulated with such sharpness and distinctness as to almost make the impression of a very fine and light *staccato*.

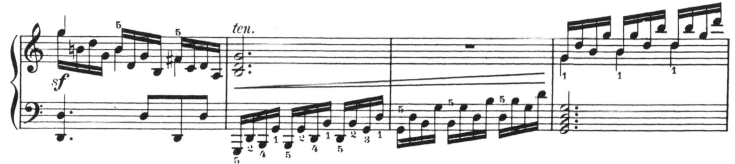

4.

*) Die äusserste Präcision im Zurück-ziehen des Fingers der rechten Hand, namentlich des dritten, ist in diesem, wie in allen analogen Takten uner-lässlich.

*) *Dans cette mesure, comme dans tou-tes celles analogues, il est absolument indispensable d'observer l'exactitude la plus rigoureuse en levant les doigts de la main droite (principalement le troi-sième doigt).*

*) Extreme precision in drawing back the fingers of the right hand, especially the 3d, is absolutely necessary in this and all analogous measures.

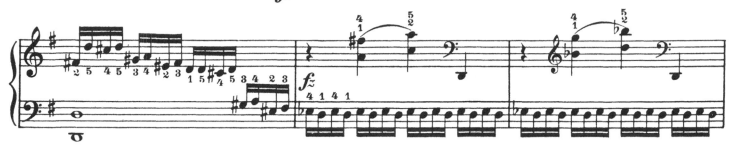

*) Der eigenthümliche Fingersatz bringt nur dann Nutzen, wenn der vierte Finger möglichst gekrümmt aufgesetzt wird.

*) Un doigté semblable n'aura son utilité qu'en levant et recourbant le plus possible le quatrième doigt.

*) The peculiar fingering is of advantage only when the 4th finger strikes curved as much as possible.

Bizzarria vivace.

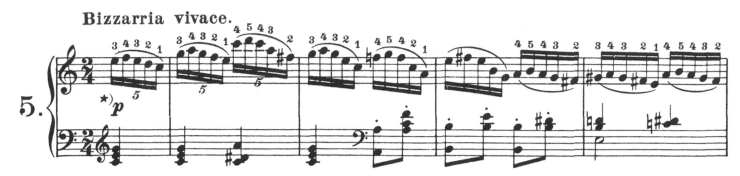

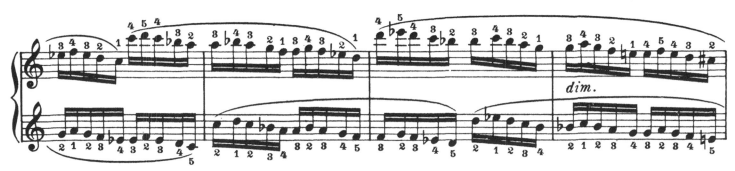

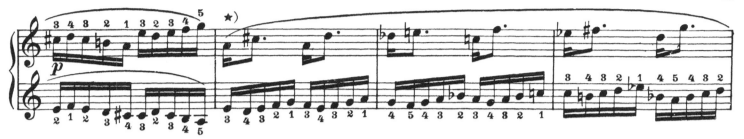

stacc. il basso

*) Die Stelle ist so auszuführen: *) *Exécutez ce passage de la façon suivante:*   *) Play this passage thus:

Allegro molto vivace.

6.

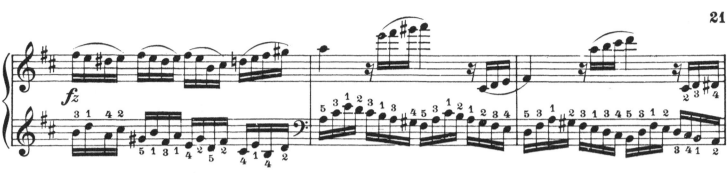

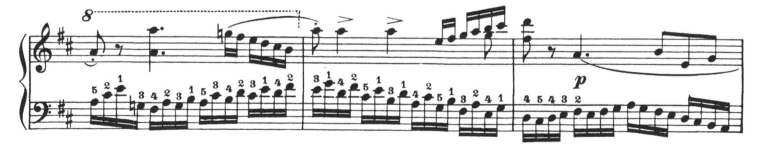

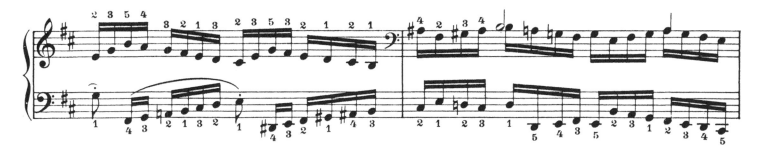

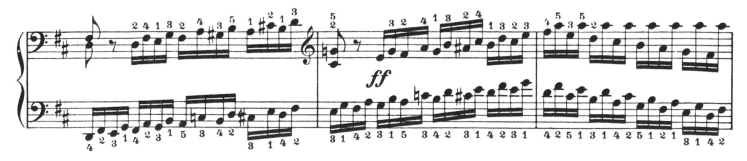

7.

Vivace non troppo.

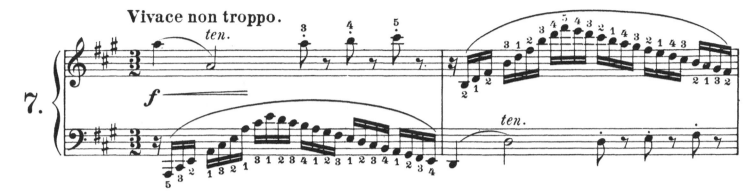

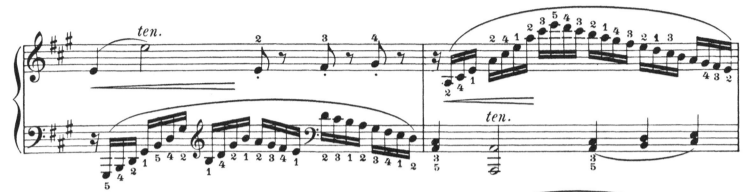

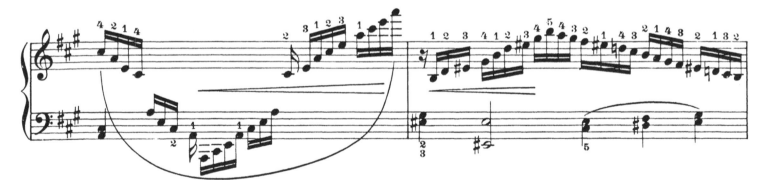

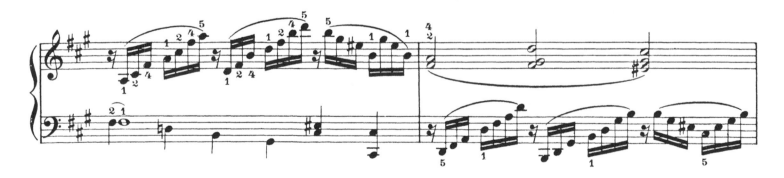

Vivacissimo.

8.

*) Es ist zweckmässig, die Takte 1, 3, 5, 7,
8, 9, 10, 11 u.s.w. zu verdoppeln; z. B:

*) *Il sera bon de redoubler les mesures 1,
3, 5, 7, 8, 9, 10, 11 etc., par exemple:*

*) It will be advantageous to double meas-
ures 1, 3, 5, 7, 8, 9, 10, 11, etc., thus:

u.s.w.
etc.

28

Presto.

9.

*) Die ersten vier Noten jedes Taktes | *) *Jouez staccato les quatre premieres* | *) The first four notes of each measure
sind gestossen zu üben: | *notes de chaque mesure:* | should be practised *staccato:*

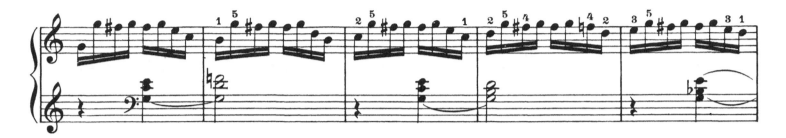

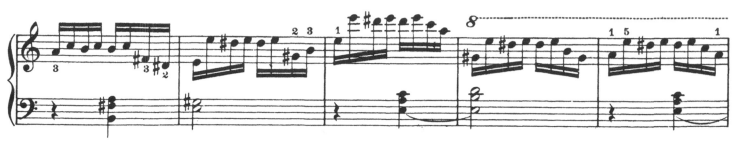

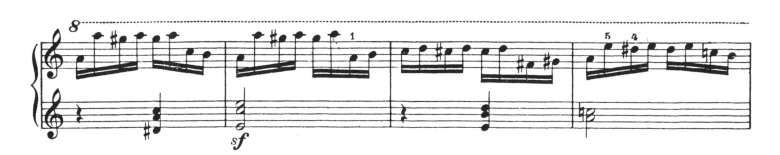

Allegretto con espressione.

10.

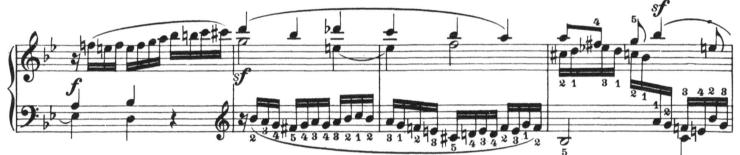

Allegro.

11.

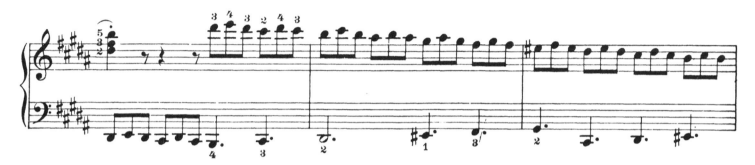

Allegro con molto brio.

12.

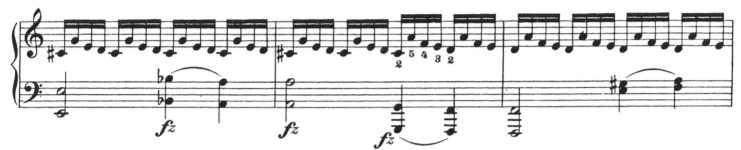

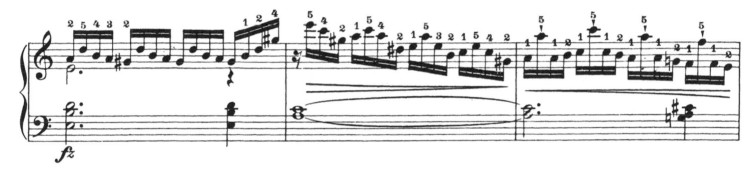

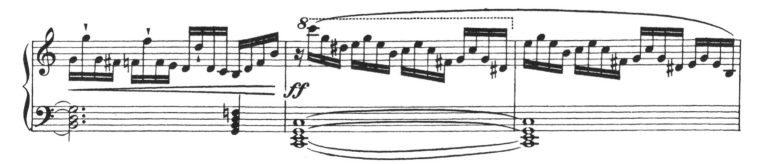

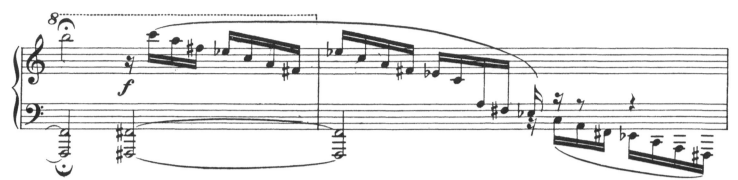

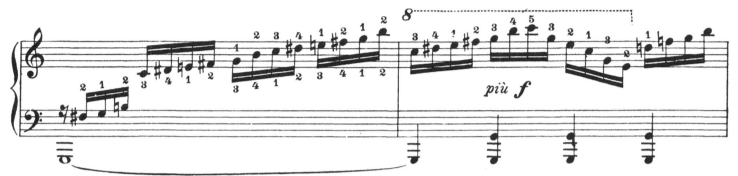

Allegrissimo.

13.

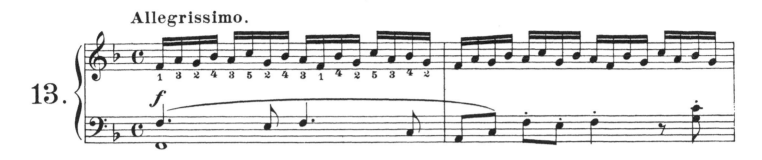

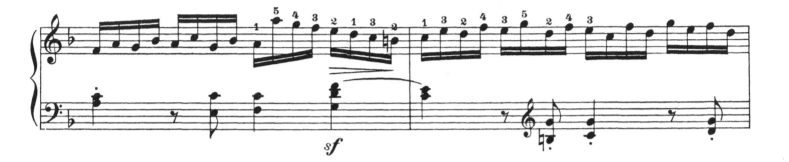

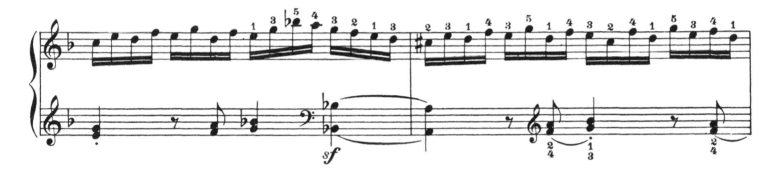

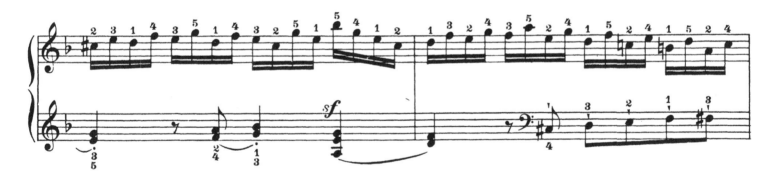

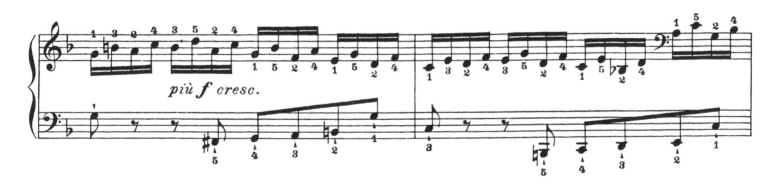

Vivace.

14.

48

Allegrissimo.

15.

*) Sämmtliche 16^{tel} werden in dieser Etüde gestossen geübt. Der Vorschlag darf durchaus nicht mit der ersten Note jedes Viertels zusammen fallen, sondern muss selbstständig abgestossen werden.

*) Dans cette étude chaque seizième de note sera joué staccato. La petite note (acciaccature) ne doit pas se jouer en même temps que chaque quart de note, mais au contraire être détachée d'une façon indépendante.

*) All the 16th-notes are to be practised staccato in this Étude. The appoggiatura must by no means be struck together with the first 16th-note of each beat, but staccato by itself.

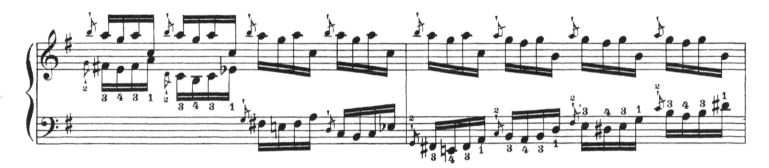

16.

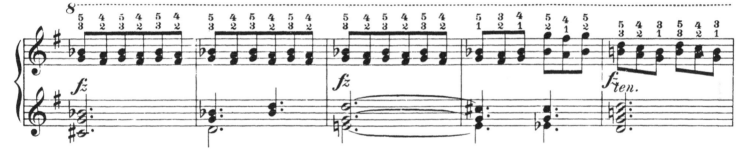

Vivacissimo.

17.

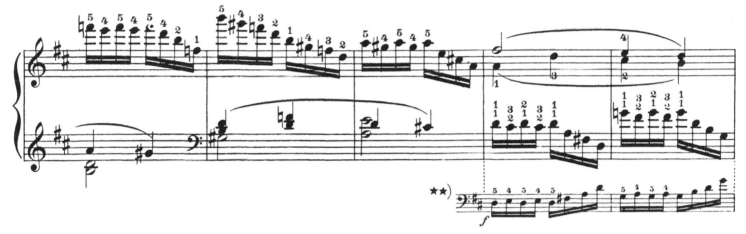

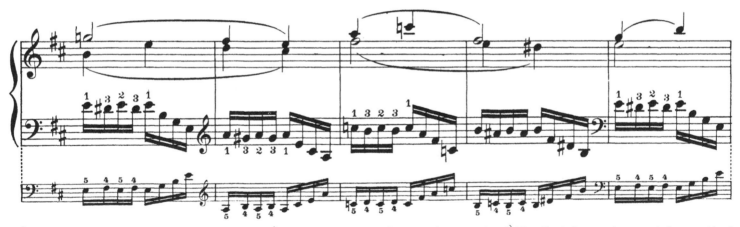

*) Die ersten vier Noten sind staccato zu üben:

*) *Les quatre premières notes sont à jouer staccato:*

*) The first four notes are to be practised *staccato:*

**) Es ist von Nutzen, die zweite Version zu üben, zur Kräftigung des vierten und fünften Fingers der linken Hand.

**) *Pour développer la force des quatrième et cinquième doigts de la main gauche il sera utile d'exercer aussi la seconde version.*

**) It will be useful to practise the second version, for strengthening the 4th and 5th fingers of the left hand.

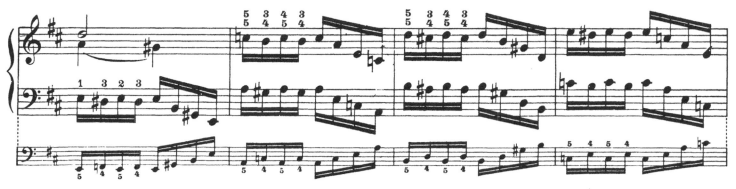

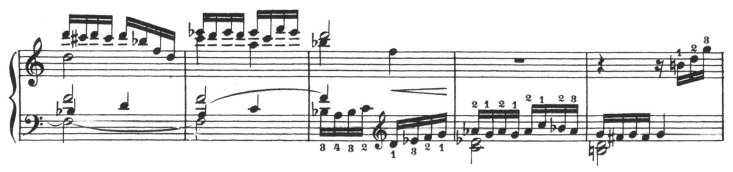

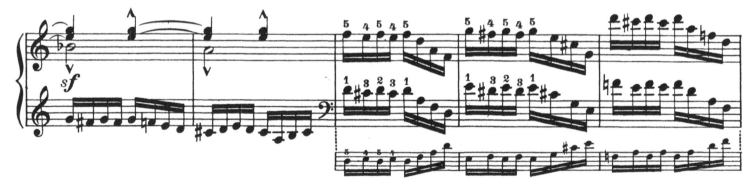

Presto non troppo.

18.

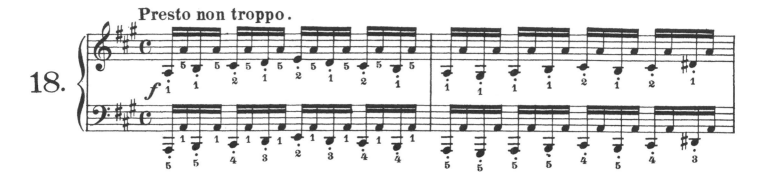

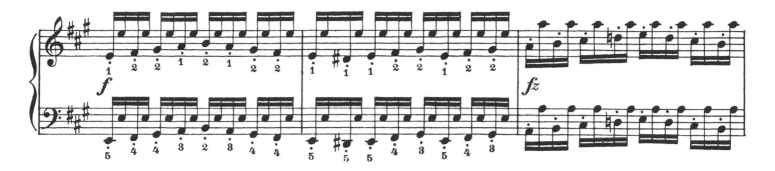

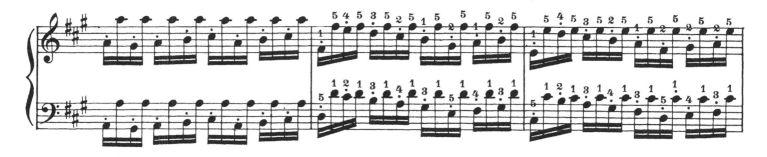

Es ist zweckmässig, folgende Stellen auch mit einem andern Fingersatz zu üben.

Il sera bon d'exercer les passages suivants avec un autre doigté.

It is advisable also to practise the following passages with another fingering.

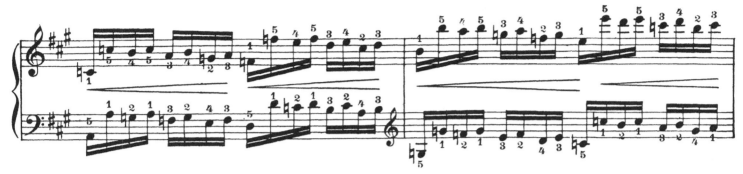

Presto.

19.

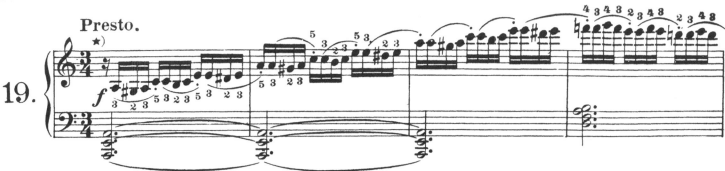

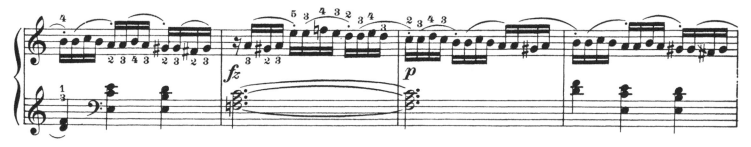

*) Zur besondern Kräftigung des **4ten** und **5ten** Fingers ist diese Etüde mit folgendem Fingersatz zu üben:

Avec le doigté indiqué ci-dessous, cette étude servira à augmenter la force des quatrième et cinquième doigts.

For specially strengthening the **4th** and **5th** fingers, this Étude should be practised with the following fingering:

u.s.w.
etc.

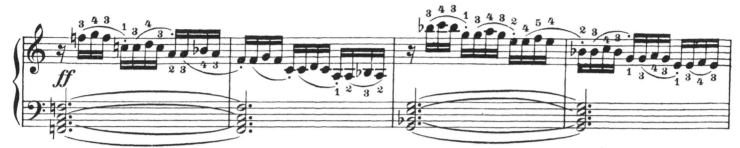

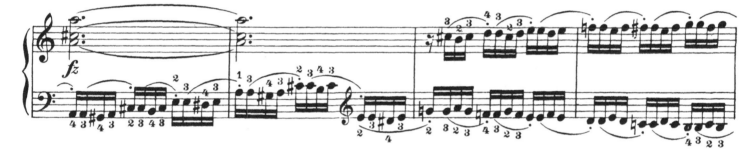

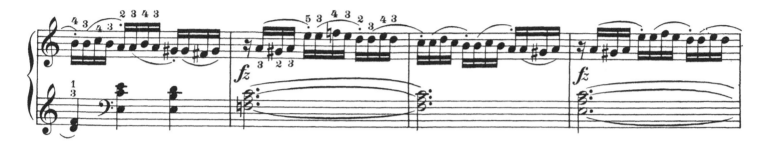

Presto.

20.

legato

Es ist zweckmässig, bei dem Studium dieser Etüde den Accent abwechselnd auf die erste, zweite und dritte Note fallen zu lassen; z.B.:

En exerçant cette étude il sera avantageux de faire tomber l'accent tour à tour sur la première, la seconde, ou la troisième note.

When practising this Etude it is advisable to play it through at first with the accent on the first note of each group, the next time on the second, and lastly on the third.

Allegro.

21.

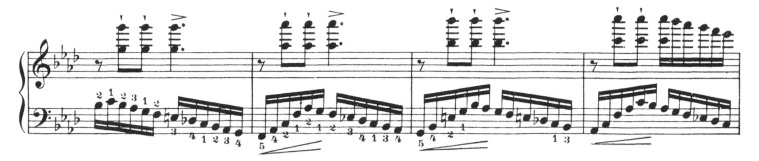

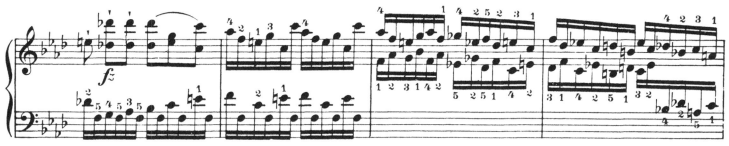

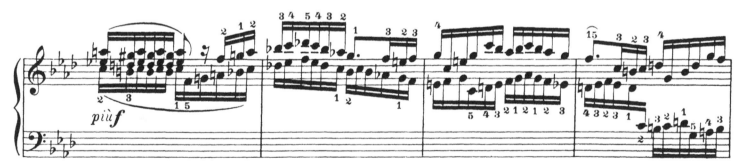

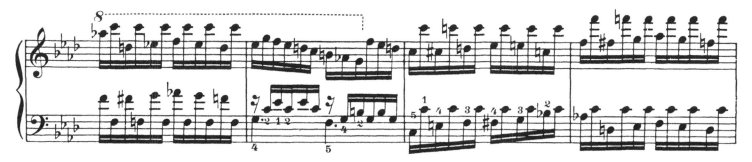

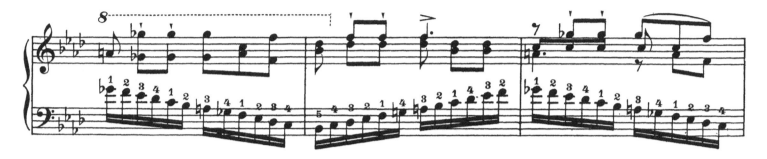

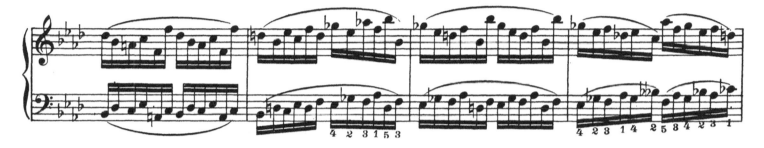

Allegro con fuoco.

22.

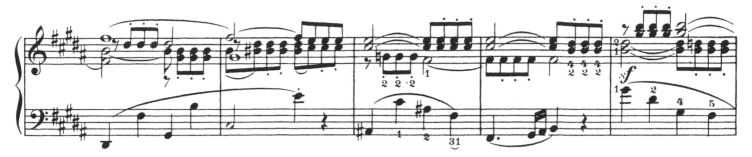

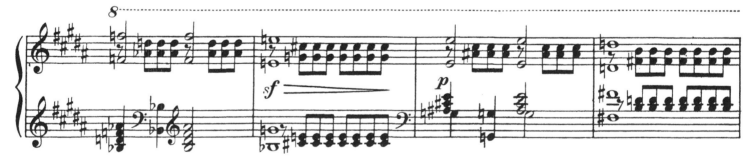

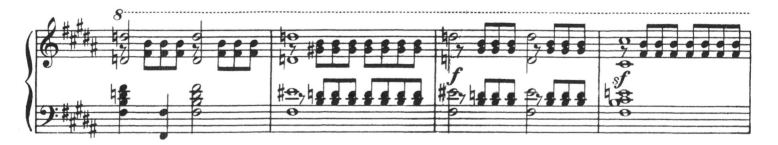

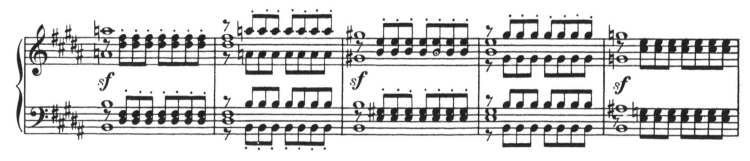

Veloce.

23.

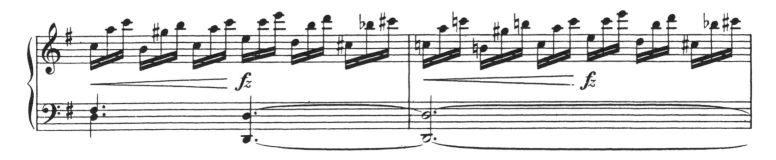

Presto.

24.

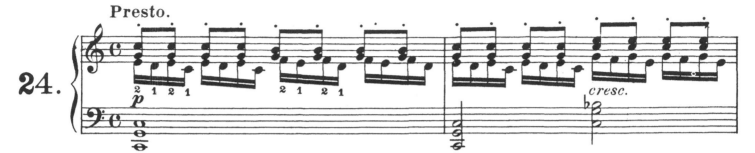

Molto allegro.

25.

*) Diese Übung muss mindestens dreimal gleich hintereinander wiederholt werden.

*) Répétez cet exercice trois fois de suite au moins.

*) This Étude should be repeated at least three times in immediate succession.

Allegro vigoroso.

26.

*) **f** *staccato*

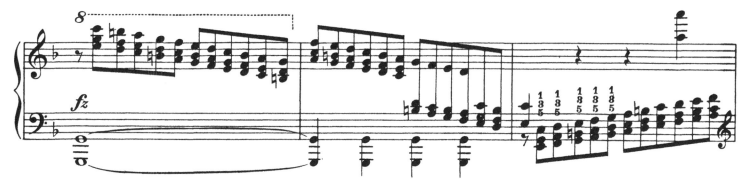

*)Die Octaven sind mit dem Hand-
gelenk zu üben.

*)*Travaillez les octaves du poignet.*

*)The Octaves are to be practised with
the wrist-stroke.

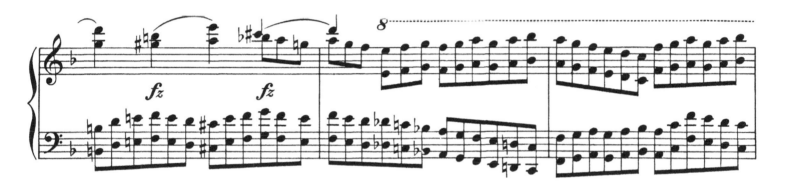

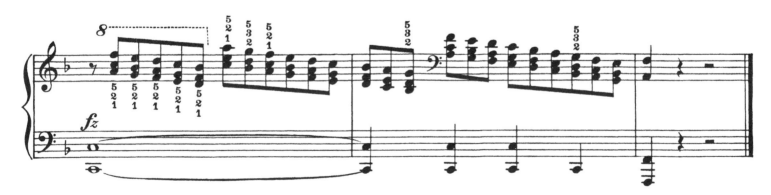

27.

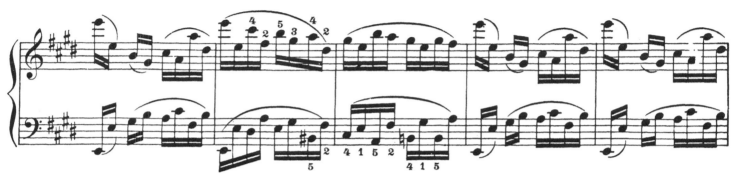

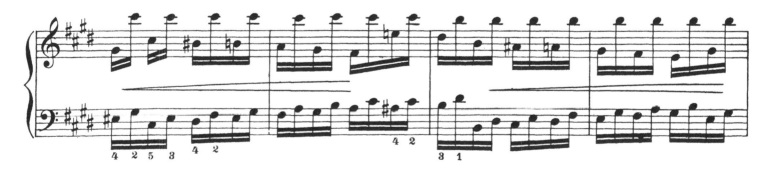

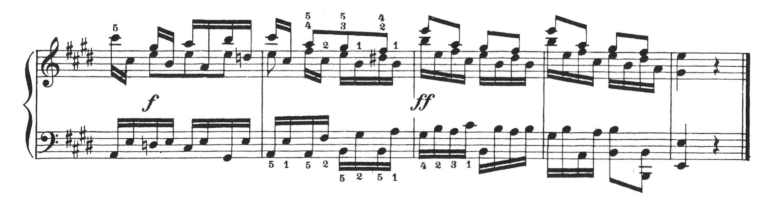

28.

*) Diese Etüde muss mindestens dreimàl gleich hintereinander wiederholt wer - den. Der Daumen der rechten und der fünfte Finger der linken Hand sollen scharf abgestossen werden.

*) *Répétez cette étude trois fois de suite au moins, en détachant fortement le pouce de la main droite et le cinquième doigt de la main gauche.*

*) Play this Étude through at least three times in uninterrupted succession. The thumb of the right hand and the **5th** finger of the left must play **sharply staccato**.

Allegro con spirito.

29.

*) In dieser Etüde muss der zweite Finger und der Daumen der rechten Hand scharf abgestossen werden.

*) Travaillez cette étude en détachant fortement le second doigt et le pouce de la main droite.

*) In this Étude the 2nd finger and thumb of the right hand should play sharply staccato.

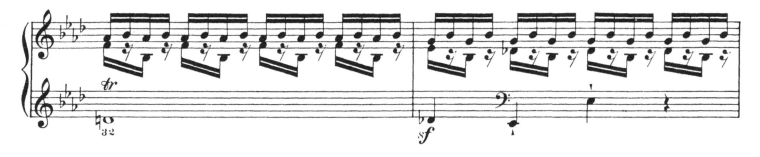

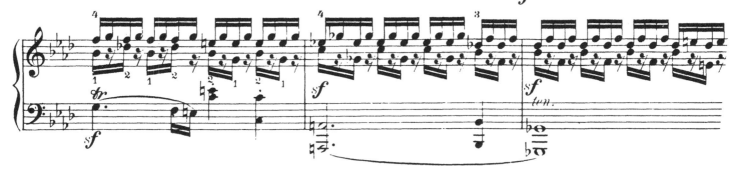

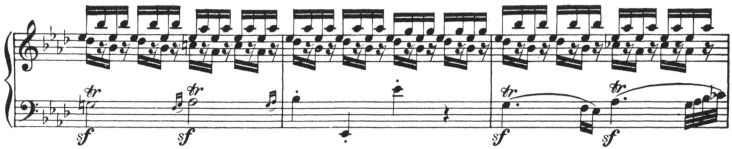

Terzen-Scalen
in allen Dur- und Molltonarten.

Gammes en Tierces
en tous les tons majeurs et mineurs.

Scales in Thirds
in all the major and minor keys.

Carl Tausig.

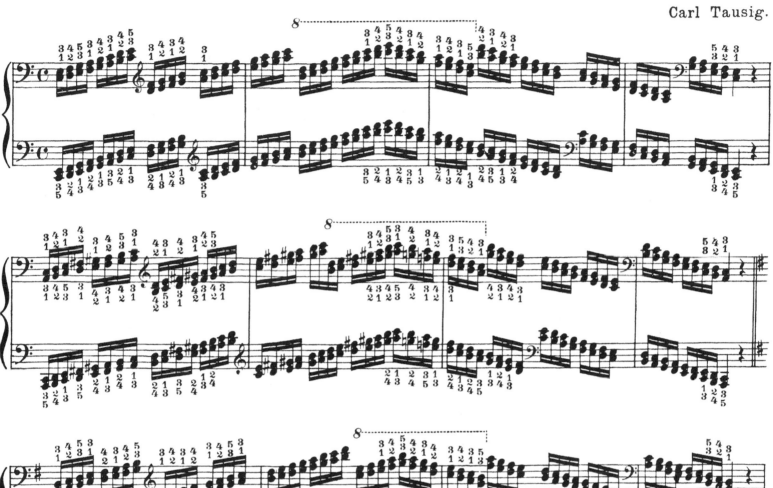

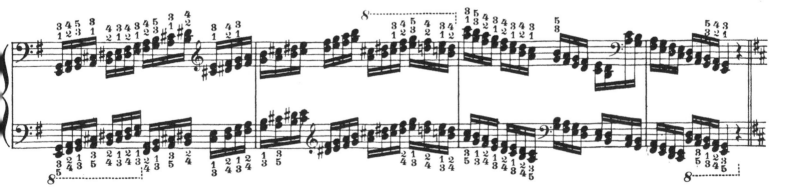

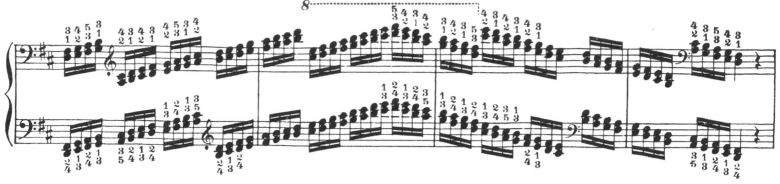

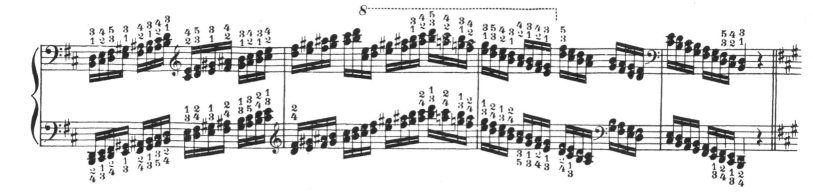

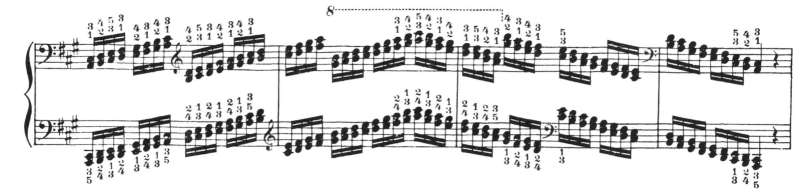

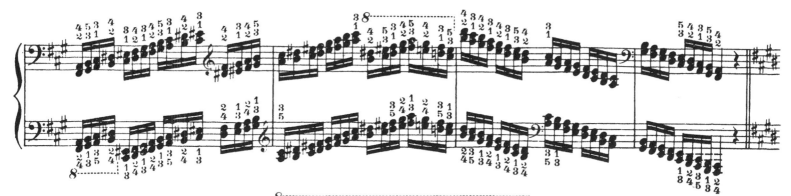

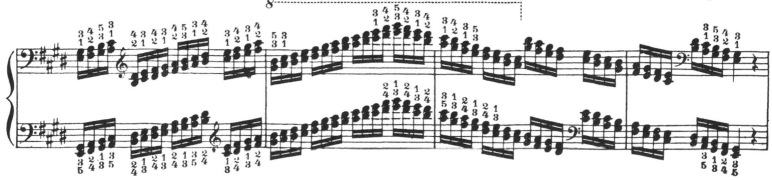

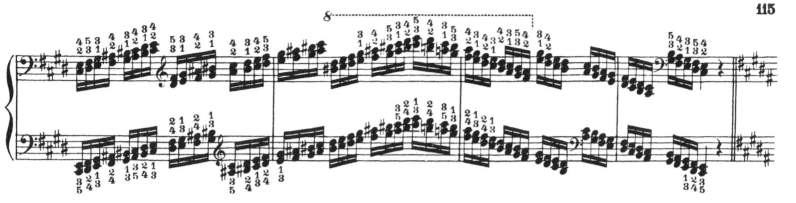

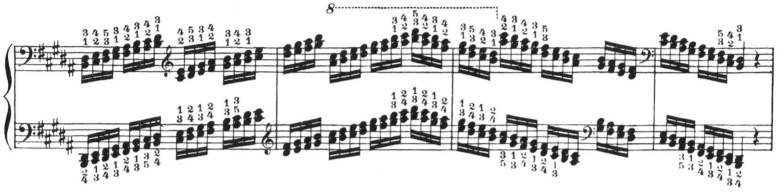

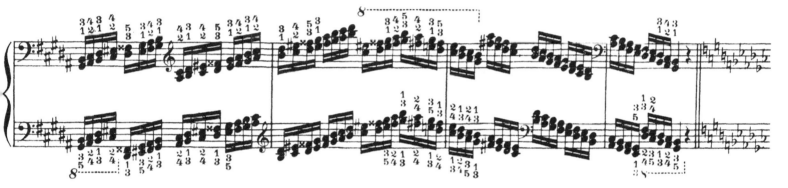

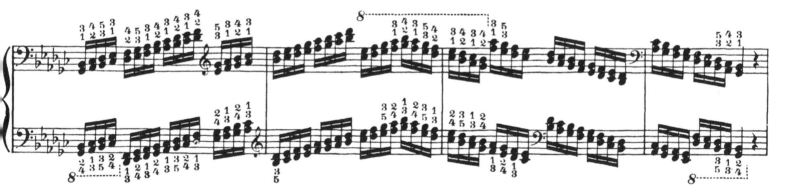

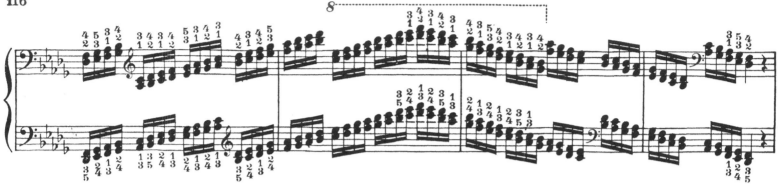

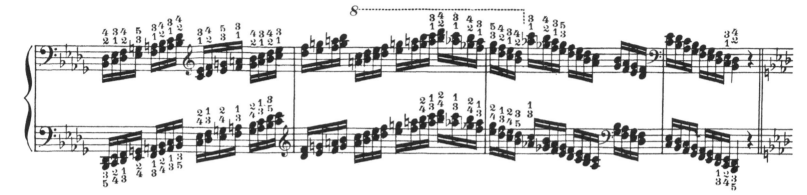

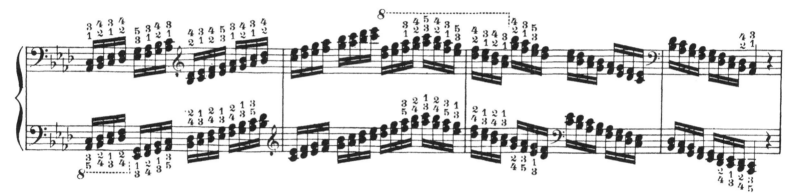

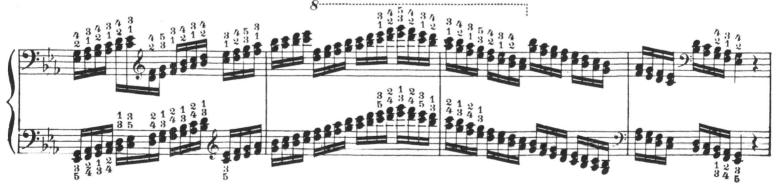

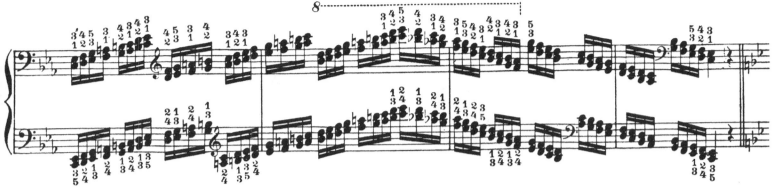

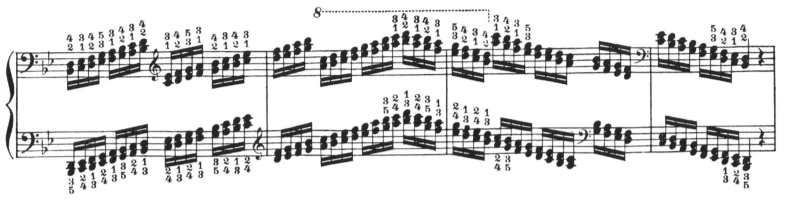

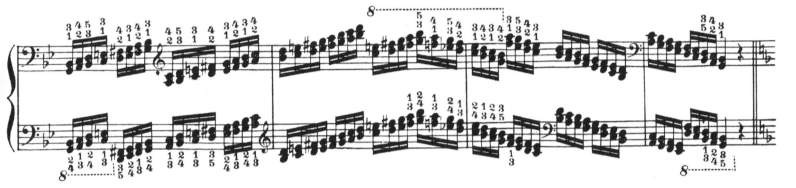

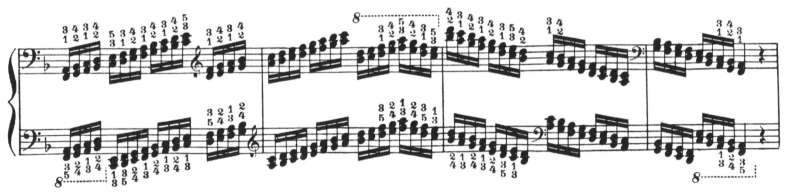

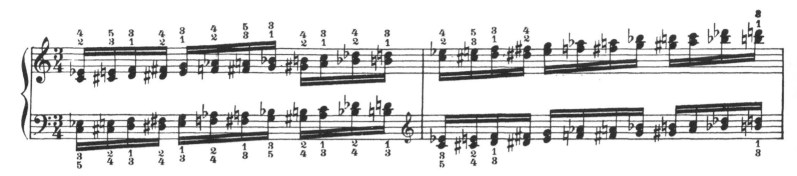

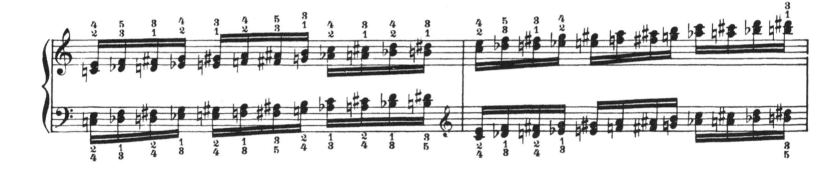

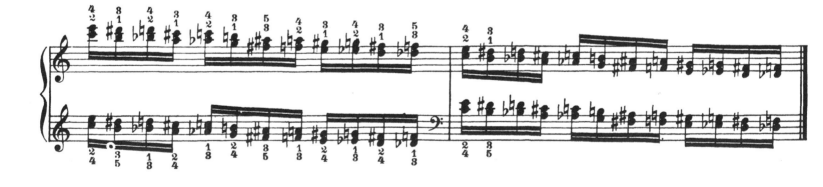